THE DAY MARTIN-BAKER SAVED MY LIFE

The True Account of a Miraculous Escape
from a Burning Navy Fighter

WILLIAM WALTHALL
FORMER LIEUTENANT, USNR

The Day Martin-Baker Saved My Life by William Walthall
Copyright © 2024 by William Walthall
All Rights Reserved.
ISBN: 978-1-59755-812-9

Published by: ADVANTAGE BOOKS™
                Orlando, FL
                www.advbookstore.com

All Rights Reserved. This book and parts thereof may not be reproduced in any form, stored in a retrieval system or transmitted in any form by any means (electronic, mechanical, photocopy, recording or otherwise) without prior written permission of the author, except as provided by United States of America copyright law.

Name:	Walthall, William
Title:	The Day Martin-Baker Saved My Life
	William Walthall, Author
	Advantage Books, 2024
Identifiers:	ISBN Paperback: 978159758129
Subjects:	BOOKS: Biographies & Memoirs
	BOOKS: Biographies & Memoirs - Survival
	BOOKS: Military – Biographies & Personal Narratives – Branches – Navy

First Printing: October 2024
24 25 26 27 28 29   10 9 8 7 6 5 4 3 2 1

Table of Contents

DEDICATION 5

CHAPTER 1: A FIRE IN YOUR PLANE IS NEVER A GOOD THING 7

CHAPTER 2: MY VISIT TO THE COMPANY THAT SAVED MY LIFE 15

CHAPTER 3: THE ESCAPE 21

CHAPTER 4: THE DREAM 29

ACKNOWLEDGMENTS 34

REFERENCES 36

William Walthall

The Day Martin-Baker Saved My Life

Dedication

This book is dedicated to my good friend, Bryson Thompson. Bryson was my pilot on the day of the accident. He had the courage and the restraint to stay at the controls of the burning Navy F-4 Phantom while I was trapped in the back cockpit and unable to eject in a normal manner.

Thanks, Bryson, for hanging in there.

William Walthall

Chapter 1

A Fire in Your Plane Is Never a Good Thing

It was *not* a dark and stormy night over the Gulf of Tonkin. Nor were we streaking across North Vietnam dodging blistering anti-aircraft fire and lethal surface-to-air missiles—that was just a few months away. On this warm, sunny Friday in mid-April 1965, my pilot and I were cruising over a barren Southern California desert en route to a remote military aerial bombing and gunnery range. Without opposition of any sort, it seemed like a perfect day to practice dropping 250-pound general-purpose bombs.

But first, let me provide the background for April 16.

After a year of training as a Navy officer and in navigation and weapons systems, I joined my operational squadron, VF-161, home-based at Miramar Naval Air Station north of San Diego. VF-161, call sign "Rock River," had recently transitioned from the F-3 "Demon" to the new McDonnell Douglas F-4 "Phantom." As a supersonic, high-altitude, air-to-air interceptor, the Phantom was specifically designed to bring down Russian bombers capable of carrying nuclear warheads. At the time, the F-4 was the world's fastest production fighter, even faster than many of today's Generation 5 fighters. Although primarily an interceptor, the Phantom was also capable of fulfilling an air-to-ground role: dropping bombs and firing Zuni rockets in close-air support.

The Phantom was a two-seater arranged in tandem. In the Navy version, only the pilot in the front seat had flight controls. The "back-seater," where I sat, was designated Radar Intercept Officer, or "RIO." We were trained to operate the radar for the weapons system and assist the pilot with navigation and communications. Therefore, RIOs required only abbreviated training compared to pilots.

When arriving at the squadron, I was assigned to fly with Lieutenant Junior Grade (JG) Bryson Thompson, a veteran pilot who had been on the ground floor of VF-161's transition from F-3s to F-4s. Bryce, as I called him, had already made one brief cruise to the Pacific and was an experienced naval aviator. It was an excellent pairing for a young, naive Ensign RIO like me with no operational experience. Bryson had been there, done that.

My call sign was "Walls." On intercept missions, my role as an RIO was to acquire the enemy airplane on the radar, lock it up, and direct the pilot to the ideal intercept point where he could fire a Sparrow missile to annihilate the enemy bomber. During air-to-ground

The Day Martin-Baker Saved My Life

bombing missions, however, my responsibility was to call out altitudes to the pilot so he could focus his attention on the target. Our tactic on this April 16 mission was to simulate evading enemy radar by making a high-speed, low-altitude approach and, a few miles from the target, pop up to fifteen thousand feet or so, roll over, and dive down on the target at about a seventy-degree angle.

That was the briefing, anyway.

The takeoff from Miramar NAS (Naval Air Station) and the flight to the Yuma bombing range were routine in every respect. With our wingman alongside, we made our way across the barren desert, eventually being handed off by the flight controllers to the bombing range. However, about ten miles from the target, Bryce and I heard a loud "thump" in the Phantom, somewhere in the fuselage behind my ejection seat. Our first thought was that we had experienced a "bird strike," a particular problem when flying nearly supersonic just a few hundred feet off the ground. The F-4 had two large air intakes which were like gargantuan mouths ready to gulp any foreign object that strayed near them. Uncertain of what caused the noise in the back of the plane, we had our wingman check us over.

"Everything looks okay," he radioed.

"Roger that," Bryce said, "but I think we'll head back to Miramar and have the plane checked over. It was pretty loud."

"Do you want us to follow you?"

"Negative. Go on to the target. See you back at Miramar."

"Roger."

Our wingman peeled off and headed back to the bombing range.

We had left the desert and were cruising over farmland at about five thousand feet when, suddenly, the right engine fire warning light lit up.

"We've got a fire warning light in the right engine," Bryce said. "The EGT's climbing. Some of my instruments are going haywire. I'm shutting down the engine." (The EGT gauge indicated "exhaust gas temperature" and was confirmation that the engine was on fire.) Shutting down an engine due to a fire was standard procedure, as the General Electric J79 engines were not equipped with fire retardant or extinguishing systems. Bryson hoped that shutting down the engine would starve it of fuel and allow the airflow to extinguish the fire. One engine was powerful enough to keep the airplane flying and make a safe landing.

The Day Martin-Baker Saved My Life

No sooner had Bryce said that than two disturbing things happened. First, the circuit breaker panel in the rear cockpit near my right leg started popping breakers so fast I couldn't keep count, much less determine which circuits were affected. The second problem—and most concerning—was that our cockpits began filling with smoke. Bryce looked down and saw flames *now coming out of both intakes!*

Simultaneously, the left engine fire warning light came on.

"We've got another fire warning light!" Bryce said. "We're going to have to eject," Bryce said as he shut down the left engine. Then, the controls froze. We had no choice—our brand-new F-4 Phantom was about to become a pile of rubble in some fine farmer's alfalfa field east of El Centro.

In the F-4 Phantom, the crewman in the back seat, the RIO, always ejected first. That was to protect him. If the pilot ejected first, not only would control of the Phantom be lost, but the fire and blast from his ejection seat could also burn the back seater. As stated earlier, unlike the Air Force Phantoms, no flight controls were in the back seat.

"Do you want me to eject?" I asked as calmly as I could.

There was a slight hesitation as Bryce had to make the excruciating decision if he was about to turn a brand-new, multi-million-dollar Phantom into expensive debris. Finally, Bryce commanded, "Eject, eject, eject!"

The standard procedure for using an ejection seat, to which we were always securely strapped in, is to reach up with both hands, grasp the handles above the helmet at the top of the seat, and pull down on the "face curtain." The curtain comes down over the face of the crewman to protect him from debris, fire, and air blast. When the curtain is pulled down, an initiator is fired, triggering a pneumatic system that causes the canopy to unlock and raise up. Small thrusters assist the airstream in blowing the canopy off the airplane. For obvious reasons, safety systems required the thick plexiglass canopy to be jettisoned before the ejection seat would fire.

So, with a load of adrenaline rushing through my body, I reached up, grabbed the ejection seat handles, and pulled down hard, just as I had practiced in training.

The curtain came down about halfway ... *and stopped!* I pulled again, harder. Nothing happened! The problem was immediately obvious to me—the curtain wouldn't come down all the way and eject the seat because the canopy didn't jettison.

For this particular problem, I hadn't been trained, but at least I realized immediately that the seat didn't fire because the canopy didn't jettison. Unbelievably, I had gone through this scenario in my mind dozens of times:

The Day Martin-Baker Saved My Life

"What if the canopy doesn't open automatically like it's supposed to do when I pull the curtain?" So I knew what to do next: I reached up with my gloved left hand for the yellow Emergency Canopy Release Handle and pulled it back as hard as possible, assuming the air stream would blow the canopy off once it popped up. The handle instantly rotated back all the way, just like it had done in training ... *but nothing happened!* I pulled it back several times with the same result: the Emergency Canopy Release mechanism wasn't working either! As long as the canopy was still down and locked, the ejection seat would not fire, and there was no getting out of the Phantom with the canopy still on.

By this time, we were descending in a rapid glide, as Bryce had shut down both engines. (The word "glide" is used loosely here; the F-4 could "glide" about as well as a twenty-two-ton granite boulder.)

"What's going on back there?" Bryce asked calmly.

"I can't get my damn canopy off!"

"Try the Emergency Canopy Release Handle," he suggested.

"I did. It's not working either."

I had one option left—the Manual Canopy Unlock Handle located on the right side of the cockpit. It was essentially a mechanical lever designed to break the canopy hinges. Once the hinges were broken, the canopy would pop up and the airstream would blow it off. There was only one problem: if there was *any* air pressure in the canopy pneumatic lines, the Manual Canopy Unlock Handle was prevented from functioning, and the hinges could not be broken.

But this was my last alternative. I reached up with my right hand, grasped the Manual Canopy Unlock Handle, and pulled it back until it stopped.

Nothing! The canopy remained down and locked.

At this point, to say that I was concerned is an understatement. Terrified would be a better choice of words. In the amount of time Bryce recited the ejection sequence to me, I had repeated the entire cycle three times in case I missed something. The result was the same ... I was trapped! Everything I had tried to open my canopy had failed, and with the canopy still on, there was no way the ejection seat would fire. We were rapidly descending toward a bright green alfalfa field in a high-performance, state-of-the-art jet fighter that was out of control, on fire, and full of fuel and bombs.

I was trapped in my cockpit ... and Bryce stayed with me.

Chapter 2

My Visit to the Company That Saved My Life

In July 2024, nearly sixty years after the accident, my wife, Nancy, and I flew to England to visit the Martin-Baker factory. It is located in Higher Denham, Uxbridge, Middlesex, about a 45-minute train ride west of London. Here is the Wikipedia blurb on Martin-Baker:

> **Martin-Baker Aircraft Company Limited** is a British manufacturer of ejection seats and safety-related equipment for aviation. The company was originally an aircraft manufacturer before becoming a pioneer in the field of ejection seats....

> Martin-Baker supplies ejection seats for 93 air forces worldwide. Martin-Baker seats have been fitted into over 200 fixed-wing and rotary types with the most recent being the Lockheed Martin F-35 Lightning II programme.

Martin-Baker claimed in 2022 that since the first live ejection test in 1945, a total of 7,674 lives have been saved by the company's ejection seats.

(Wikipedia contributors, "Martin-Baker," *Wikipedia, The Free Encyclopedia,*

https://en.wikipedia.org/w/index.php?title=Martin-Baker&oldid=1241242632

(accessed August 21, 2024).

Nancy and I left Los Angeles International on the evening of July 1st and landed at Gatwick Airport the next day. We stayed at a B&B for a few days and toured London before traveling to Martin-Baker for our scheduled visit.

From the Victoria station, we made our way through England's excellent rail system, eventually getting off the train at a small stop called Denham Golf Club, just past the little village of Denham in Buckinghamshire. It was pouring rain, and there was not a soul around. At least we had raincoats, so we huddled under an overpass, hoping the rain would stop. Fortunately, a lovely lady with her Golden Retriever emerged from a field and directed us to the Martin-Baker factory. Walking down the road toward the factory, by now soaked, a gentleman in a black four-door SUV stopped and asked if we needed a ride. It turned out that he worked at Martin-Baker.

The most striking feature to me was that from the front, the Martin-Baker facilities looked nothing like what I expected a world-renowned factory would look like. We could easily have walked right by the factory and never realized how important this place was! The facilities are, in fact, sprawling, yet the buildings were utterly unassuming in all respects. Mostly single-story brick with slightly gabled roofs, you would think it is just a group of storage or small manufacturing buildings. I saw this as a testimony to manufacturing efficiency.

After being cleared at the guardhouse—the guard had our names on a list of visitors—we were escorted into the front reception area. We were soon greeted by our host, Tony Gaunt.

You will never meet a nicer person than Tony Gaunt. Extremely friendly and hospitable, Tony has spent years with Martin-Baker in various roles and is now "Principal Technical Advisor." Tony knew Martin-Baker inside and out and was the perfect person to take us on our tour, which lasted *almost two hours*. Tony walked us through every part of the manufacturing and assembly process of putting together ejection seats. Nancy and I were awed at the complexity and degree of detail in manufacturing, assembling, testing, and installing these life-saving seats. We toured several buildings, including the parachute packing room, which we could observe only at a distance for safety reasons. I was shocked at how much pressure it takes to cram a packed parachute and its drogue chute into the small "chute box" ... about three thousand pounds.

Of particular interest was a room showing the evolution of ejection seats. There, situated toward the front, was a Mk. H5 ejection seat (Mk5 for short), the model Bryce and I were sitting on when our plane caught fire. Of course, when I was in the Navy, it was just "the ejection seat" inside a cramped cockpit. The only thing I needed to know then was how to use it, and I knew none of the details of the meticulous manufacturing that went into it. Tony explained that the Mk5 seat could be safely fired at ground level "if the plane was moving forward" at a good speed. Later models are so powerful that the plane can be parked on the ground (or carrier) and be fired safely.

Tony stated that other companies manufacture ejection seats, but Martin-Baker has the lion's share, particularly in the United States and the United Kingdom.

Another highlight occurred as we were heading back to the reception area. Tony took us into a separate building where we had the privilege of meeting none other than Andrew Martin himself, one of the co-founders of Martin-Baker Aircraft Company. As stated earlier, when Martin-Baker first started in 1945, they manufactured a few aircraft but soon focused entirely

The Day Martin-Baker Saved My Life

on ejection seats as jet aircraft were coming of age. Andrew Martin is as stately a gentleman as you will ever meet. Dressed in a dark blue suit and Martin-Baker tie, he greeted Nancy and me warmly, shaking our hands with genuine sincerity and interest. As busy as he was, he took the time to listen intently to my own ejection story. I'm sure it was just one of many stories he had heard from the *thousands* of lives his vision and dedication had saved. Tony, of course, took a photo.

After completing our factory tour, Tony took us back to the reception room. On the back wall of the reception room are the names of all those who have ejected with a Martin-Baker seat. My pilot, Bryson, had toured Martin-Baker a few years earlier and found our numbers: 760 and 761. Tony had the receptionist take a picture of the two of us, with me pointing high to my number, 760. To put that number in perspective, the latest count of pilots saved with Martin-Baker seats is *over 7700*; that placed Bryson and me in the first ten percent of lives saved. Tony, the guards at the reception desk, and our extremely helpful contact person, Emma Sutcliffe, gathered around as I related my own ejection story.

Before departing Martin-Baker, Nancy and I were gifted with a variety of memorabilia: pens, patches, key rings, lapel pins, a recognition letter from Martin-Baker, and a tie with a certificate that I was now part of the "Martin-Baker Tie Club," signed by Andrew Martin himself.

There was still a drizzle when Tony dropped us off at the train station in Denham. After he departed, we discovered from the ticket booth that we had just missed the return train to London. The next train was over an hour later. Fortunately, Tony had given us a Martin-Baker umbrella! So, in the misty drizzle, Nancy and I walked the quarter mile to the little village of Denham, where we found a delightful cafe and, of course, ordered bangers and mash with peas. What else?

Our day was complete. It goes without saying that our visit to Martin-Baker, the primary reason for traveling to England, was the highlight of our trip.

Now, back to the day of the crash...

Chapter 3

The Escape

So, there I was, fast descending toward an alfalfa field near El Centro, California, trapped in the back seat of a high-performance, state-of-the-art jet fighter that was out of control, on fire, and full of fuel and bombs.

As I recounted in Chapter 1, I had made all the right moves to jettison the back canopy and fire the Martin-Baker ejection seat, all without success. Bryce was anxiously waiting for me to eject so that he, too, could exit from the doomed Phantom, which was now only five hundred feet above the ground.

It is difficult to remember all that was going through my mind at the time. I was intensely focused on getting the canopy off so I could eject from the Phantom. Everything I had been trained to do failed. All alternatives seemed fruitless. I felt an overwhelming sense of frustration and confusion, if not anger—nothing was working as it should. I was on the verge of panic, and my demise seemed imminent. Ironically, I had, on occasion, imagined scenarios like this in my mind; that is, finding myself in an untenable situation in the Phantom and facing imminent death. As a young Christian, I had always thought that if I ever got into a situation like this, that is, coming face-to-face with impending death, I would joyfully raise my eyes to heaven and pray, "Well, God, it's been a great ride. Thank you for all your blessings. I've had a good life. Now, I am ready to come into your presence." But that is *not* what I was thinking. What I really whispered under my breath was, "God! Get me out of this damn airplane!" Isn't it funny how our ideals don't always match reality?

So, after repeating the automatic ejection sequence and the backup systems several times without success, I had only one option left: try the Manual Canopy Unlock Lever one more time, hoping that it would somehow pop open the canopy. As a last resort, with *both* hands, I reached up and pulled the lever with all my strength.

Snap!

Finally, pulling with enough force, I had rotated the lever hard enough to break the hinges. The canopy immediately popped up a few inches allowing the airstream to jettison it off the Phantom. With a 300-knot wind in my face, there was no way I was going to find the curtain, which had already been pulled halfway. Instinctively, I reached for the Alternate Ejection Handle located on the seat between my knees and pulled hard. With a loud blast, I was instantly ejected out of the cockpit.

The Day Martin-Baker Saved My Life

(Later, our Maintenance Chief informed me that simply pulling back on the Manual Canopy Unlock Handle was insufficient. After the initial stop, *a fifty-pound pull was required to break the hinges, something we had never been taught in ejection seat training*. What happened in my case was that the fire had burnt through both the normal *and* the backup pneumatic lines to the canopy—which, on the one hand, prevented the standard and emergency canopy mechanisms from functioning but, on the other hand, released the air pressure in the lines. He stated that a safety feature in the Manual Canopy Unlock system prevented the Manual Canopy Unlock system from functioning if there was *any* pressure in the canopy lines. Fortunately, the fire never burnt through Bryce's canopy lines, and shortly after me, he ejected without incident.)

The Martin-Baker ejection seat worked perfectly. I don't remember much about the actual ejection, but I do remember that my seat never tumbled—the seat normally tumbles at least once—and because we were at such a low altitude, my chute deployed immediately. The chute yanked me away from the seat, which it was designed to do, causing the seat and me to part ways.

Bryson and I reflexively deployed our life rafts as we had been trained. It must have looked a little silly to have life rafts dangling below us over farmland, but they served a purpose: they were an excellent way to tell how close we were to the ground so we could prepare for the landing.

Within seconds, I found myself standing in the middle of an alfalfa field, somewhat dazed. I looked up and saw Bryce only fifty yards or so away, getting himself out of his parachute harness. About a mile away, a pillar of smoke rose from where our Phantom had crashed, leaving a 40-foot-wide crater in some very rich farmland.

I suppose that I was in a slight state of shock. Even though you go through all the training, you never really believe that you would ever have to eject ... well, during a routine training mission, anyway. (Later, in Vietnam, you realized it could happen every day!)

Incredibly, there happened to be an FBI agent who witnessed the entire event. (Why was an FBI agent out in an alfalfa field in El Centro?) He came up to Bryce and introduced himself: "Mr. Thompson, I'm Mr. Peters of the FBI. Is there anything I can do for you?" Mr. Peters arranged for us to be driven to the Naval Air Station in El Centro. After a debriefing, which included immediately writing down everything we could remember about the crash, we were flown back to Miramar in a helicopter and debriefed again. We finally rejoined our squadron mates waiting to hear our story.

The Day Martin-Baker Saved My Life

So, what caused the fire? Navy accident investigators, after gathering all the rubble of the doomed Phantom, found the smoking gun.

The Phantom was designed to have what was called a "bleed air ducting system." Bleed air is created by the engine turbine blades. This highly pressurized air operates various pneumatic systems, such as landing gear, wing slats, and boundary layer control. (Boundary layer air flows over the wings to allow for lower landing speeds.) This pressurized air is directed to various parts of the Phantom via a series of ducts. The main valve controlling the flow is called "the bleed air duct valve." In our F-4, the bleed air duct valve was manufactured with bad casting and consequently developed cracks. The valve eventually gave way, breaking into metal shards, damaging ducts, and allowing hot, high-pressure air to escape into the fuselage. This resulted in the melting of wires and fuel lines, as well as the pneumatic lines to my canopy. The hot air was close to melting the fuel bladder when we got out, which could have resulted in an explosion.

Once the cause of the fire was determined, the entire fleet of Navy F-4s was inspected and it was found that *over forty percent of F-4s had cracks in the bleed air duct valve, which pointed to a defect in the design and manufacturing process.* After our accident, "bleed air duct valve failure" became a well-known phrase among Phantom aircrews. As an Air Force Phantom pilot once told me, a bleed air duct valve failure was "...every F-4 pilot's worst nightmare." Bryson and I were just glad the accident was never attributed to "pilot error."

During our debriefing, accident investigators informed us that Bryson and I may have been the first crew to survive this type of accident, that is, bleed air duct valve failure. There had previously been seven or eight mysterious disappearances of F-4s over water, with crews lost and no resolution as to the cause. It had been speculated that failure of the primary gyroscope, another known problem in early Phantoms, may have caused some of these losses. However, the actual causes were never determined; therefore, "pilot error" was always the fallback position.

Thirteen months after our ejection incident, our squadron deployed to Vietnam aboard the USS Constellation. The "Gulf of Tonkin incident" with the USS Maddox had escalated U.S. involvement. Aircraft carriers were already on "Yankee Station" in the Gulf of Tonkin, and some Navy and Air Force Phantoms had been shot down by anti-aircraft batteries, SAM missiles, and even MiG interceptors.

I completed my tours to Vietnam with over 200 combat missions during two cruises to the Gulf of Tonkin, the first aboard the USS Constellation and the second aboard the USS Coral Sea, both now decommissioned. The closest I ever came to having to eject again was on a flak suppression mission on my second deployment. We were in a sixty-degree dive

The Day Martin-Baker Saved My Life

when a 50-caliber bullet blasted through my pilot's cockpit (the late Lieutenant Commander Gordon "Gordo" Cornell), took part of his helmet off, and lodged in the headrest of his ejection seat. If we had been going a fraction of a knot slower, the bullet would have lodged in Gordo's head. If we had been going a fraction of a knot faster, it would have lodged in *my* head.

I never had another close call in Vietnam.

Bryson had long since left the Navy and was flying for Pan Am (Pan American World Airways). He later became a Training Captain (flight instructor) on the B-747. On an interesting side note, Bryson was once deadheading on his way home and struck up a conversation with one of the crew, who was also a former Phantom pilot. They began swapping stories. When Bryson shared our ejection story and the cause of the fire, the pilot reacted by saying, "So, you're the guy!"

It seems that bleed air duct valve failures in Phantoms were so notorious that they were, in fact, "an F-4 pilot's worst nightmare."

William Walthall

Chapter 4

The Dream

You might think that this story is over, and, to some degree, it is. Yet another event makes the story even more interesting—well, to the author, anyway.

The crash happened on Friday, April 16. *The night before*, I went to bed at my usual time, having had a nice dinner and a fun evening at the Miramar Officers' Club. At about two a.m., I awoke drenched in sweat. I had just had a terrible nightmare. I dreamt that Bryce and I were on a routine training mission out over the desert when, suddenly, smoke began filling the cockpit. I knew in my dream that we were on fire. I glanced down at the circuit breaker panel and saw dozens of breakers popping. In the dream, I was in a panic. I could see my yellow-gloved left hand reaching up for the Emergency Canopy Release Handle and pulling back ... several times ... with no results. That's when I woke up screaming. No, this is not a fictional or fabricated story. I have witnesses. After breakfast on the day of the crash, I rode to the hangar with the late Bill McGuigan, a pilot, in his Corvette. I told Bill about my dream, but he just laughed it off.

When Bryce and I arrived back at the hangar from El Centro, Bill was the first to come up to me. He looked me straight in the eyes and said, "Walls, you're never going to fly with me again unless we do a dream check!" He had told others in the squadron about the dream I had told him. From that day on, the words "dream check" became part of the pre-flight checklist when I flew with any pilot.

Over the years, I have recounted the event, and the dream, to several people. Some think it was just an interesting coincidence, others are skeptical, but for my squadron mates of VF-161, there was no doubt in anyone's mind that I had a premonition and that the dream had come true in every detail.

During the rest of my time flying in the Navy, through all the training flights and two cruises to Vietnam, I had similar dreams, but nothing close to my dream before the crash.

I have often wondered why I had that dream. I've never considered myself to be a psychic, and I've never had another dream like that come true. Over the years, I asked several friends and acquaintances what they thought happened to me; that is, the dream and the premonition coming true. No one had a satisfactory answer until I had lunch with my accountant some years later. He is a devout Christian. He gave me the only explanation with which I have been satisfied. He said, "That's easy; God was preparing you. He wanted you to know that He has a plan for your life."

The Day Martin-Baker Saved My Life

It took a while, but God's plan for me became evident over the years. I later attended theology seminary, graduated with a Master of Divinity, and eventually became the pastor of a church in Redlands, California.

To this day, I do not know why God chose me to have the dream other than the probability that I needed such a dream for Him to get my attention. And perhaps, too, the dream assured me that, as I stumble through this life, I am not alone.

Bryce and me in our F4

William Walthall

Miramar Jet Fliers Safe After Crash

HOLTVILLE — A twin-engine jet fighter crashed and exploded in an alfalfa field yesterday after both engines caught fire and two Navy fliers parachuted to safety.

Neither of the fliers was injured. They were identified as the pilot, Lt. (j.g.) B. H. Thompson, 26, and copilot, Ens. W. E. Walthall, 24, both of the bachelor officers quarters at Miramar Naval Air Station. Thompson is from Woodbridge, Conn. Walthall is from South Pasadena.

A Navy spokesman said the F-B from Squadron VF 161 was en route to a target area near Holtville from Miramar when both engines burst into flames.

The two officers ejected from the craft and floated to safety. The altitude at which the trouble developed was not disclosed.

The crash occurred near the Meadows-Union Road about two miles south of Meadows-Union School. The jet fuel apparently exploded as the craft crashed and blew up, spewing wreckage for 150 yards and digging a hole about seven feet deep.

A farmer who saw the plane in difficulty said it dropped like a rock and he saw the parachutes appear in the sky.

The Day Martin-Baker Saved My Life

CRASH AFTERMATH — Debris, foreground, scattered for about a quarter of a mile when a Navy twin-engined jet fighter crashed about two miles south of Meadows Union School, near Meloland this morning. The plane landed in an open field searing about five acres of alfalfa and narrowly missing a farm house by about 100 yards. In the background is smoke rising from a crater hollowed by the burning wreckage. Both pilot and co-pilot escaped injury.

(Staff Photo)

William Walthall

Acknowledgments

First on my list of acknowledgments, of course, is Bryson Thompson. As I wrote in the book, Bryson remained at the controls of a burning, rapidly descending jet fighter while I tried to figure out how to get "the damn canopy" off. Bryson was extremely helpful in filling in the blanks in my memory and assisting with details about the accident almost sixty years ago. Bryce (as I've always called him) and I have stayed in contact. A couple of years ago, my wife and I had the pleasure of having lunch with Bryce and his lovely wife, Margie, at a local restaurant. Bryson and Margie now live in Florida.

I also want to express my sincere love and appreciation for my wife, Nancy, of fifty years. She encouraged me to attend seminary and become a pastor, a dream I had for years. She also encouraged me to travel to England and visit the Martin-Baker factory.

Also on the list of appreciation are my two daughters, Krista and Leanna, who, along with others, proofread the manuscript and provided helpful suggestions.

Lastly, to the folks at Martin-Baker Aircraft Company, Limited. Their vision for saving lives and their diligence for safety are impeccable and unmatched. To Mr.

The Day Martin-Baker Saved My Life

Andrew Martin, to Tony Gaunt, to Emma Sutcliffe, and to all those whose work has saved over 7700 lives...we *all* give thanks.

References

For more information on the Martin-Baker Aircraft Company, Inc., visit: https://martin-baker.com

For more information on Bryson Thompson's story of the ejection, visit: https://martin-baker.com/stories/lt-bryson-h-thompson/

For more information on the Martin-Baker Tie Club, visit: https://martin-baker.com/tie-club/

For more information on the Mk5 ejection seat, visit: https://martin-baker.com/ejection-seats/mk5/

William Walthall is available for interviews and author appearances. For more information, send inquiry to info@advbooks.com

Other books by the author (available on Amazon):

The Love Revelation: The Royal Law
Sierra Dawning – A Story of Love
The Range of Light – A Story of Love
The Discipler's Commentary on the Gospel of Luke

we bring dreams to life™
advbookstore.com

www.ingramcontent.com/pod-product-compliance
Lightning Source LLC
Chambersburg PA
CBHW061312040426
42444CB00010B/2603

ALEXIA'S WORLD

Thriving with Sickle Cell Disease

By

Alexia Tennent

Copyright © 2019 Alexia Tennent

All rights reserved

No part of this publication may be reproduced, stored or transmitted in any form or by any means, electronic, mechanical, photocopying, recording, scanning, or otherwise without written permission from the publisher. It is illegal to copy this book, post it to a website, or distribute it by any other means without permission

ISBN: 978-1-951844-00-4